PEOPLE PAINS

PEOPLE PAINS

*Fixing The Drama
In Your Business*

Dr. Reggie Thomas

People Pains
Fixing The Drama In Your Business

Copyright © 2023 by Dr. Reggie Thomas

All rights reserved. No part of this publication may be reproduced, distributed, or transmitted in any form or by any means, including photocopying, recording, or other electronic or mechanical methods, without the prior written permission of the author, except in the case of brief quotations embodied in critical reviews and certain other noncommercial uses permitted by copyright law.

Jones Media Publishing
10645 N. Tatum Blvd. Ste. 200-166
Phoenix, AZ 85028
www.JonesMediaPublishing.com

Disclaimer:

The author strives to be as accurate and complete as possible in the creation of this book, notwithstanding the fact that the author does not warrant or represent at any time that the contents within are accurate due to the rapidly changing nature of the Internet.

While all attempts have been made to verify information provided in this publication, the Author and the Publisher assume no responsibility and are not liable for errors, omissions, or contrary interpretation of the subject matter herein. The Author and Publisher hereby disclaim any liability, loss or damage incurred as a result of the application and utilization, whether directly or indirectly, of any information, suggestion, advice, or procedure in this book. Any perceived slights of specific persons, peoples, or organizations are unintentional.

In practical advice books, like anything else in life, there are no guarantees of income made. Readers are cautioned to rely on their own judgment about their individual circumstances to act accordingly. Readers are responsible for their own actions, choices, and results. This book is not intended for use as a source of legal, business, accounting or financial advice. All readers are advised to seek the services of competent professionals in legal, business, accounting, and finance field.

Printed in the United States of America

ISBN

978-1-948382-43-4 paperback

TABLE OF CONTENTS

Introduction vii

Chapter 1: It All Begins with the Leader............ 1

Chapter 2: Managing Difficult Personalities 11

Chapter 3: Turning Conflict into Creativity........ 23

Chapter 4: Dealing with Apathy and Low
　　　　　　Motivation 33

Chapter 5: Navigating Performance Issues 43

Chapter 6: Communication Problems 55

Chapter 7: Leading People Who Don't Want to
　　　　　　be Led 67

Chapter 8: Getting Diversity and Inclusion Right... 79

Conclusion...................................... 93

About the Author 101

INTRODUCTION

I want to begin this book by sharing a bit of my story. I had a very humble beginning in life. I was raised in a small town in west Tennessee by hard-working parents who each had blue collar jobs. We also owned land and did what I call "mini-farming" because we raised crops and livestock for food.

I was just an average kid who was slightly above average academically. When I graduated from high school, I ranked right in the middle of my class. Trust me, I was not going to give Bill Gates, Warren Buffett, Steve Jobs or Jeff Bezos any competition later in life. I was absolutely no threat to them.

Sports were big in my family. My brothers and I all played baseball. I played from the time I was 8 years old through high school. I was a good player, but never the star. I was a starter and batted second in the lineup during the regular season, but during the all-star season, I was on the bench. I wasn't the best of the best.

I also lacked self-confidence growing up; I figured I'd probably have a good life, but it was going to be pretty average. I felt that if I was an average kid, I would be an average adult.

Fast forwarding, I have lived a successful life. *Am I the smartest or most skilled in a room full of other professionals?* Probably not. But I may be the best looking... ok, I'm kidding. However, I've found success both personally and professionally over the years and for that, I am proud.

My secret sauce has not been my intellect, skills or talents. My secret sauce? My relational skills. With more than 30 years as a working professional, I've served in a variety of roles– most of them being in senior leadership and management. My colleagues have affirmed my leadership, expressing how much they enjoy working with me and under me. My secret sauce has always been my ability to relate to people, care for them and lead them to success. And I have discovered that relational skills are the most important skills for having a successful career.

Of course, this is not meant to diminish intelligence, talents, dedication and other important qualities, because you definitely need those in the workplace. But if you want to experience *professional success*, you need sharp people skills and you need to master emotional intelligence.

Dr. Daniel Goleman, an expert in the field of emotional intelligence, believes 25% of our success in life is due to our IQ (Intelligence Quotient) but 75% of our success comes from our EQ (Emotional Quotient). We must be able to connect with people on an *emotional* level.

Perhaps you're reading this book because you're a business leader. You read the title and it resonated because you are navigating the challenges of relationships within your organization or business. You already know that some relationships are easy. You have people in your organization who are easy to get along with. You connect with them and relate to them very well. They are low drama and do not create problems and conflict with you or within your organization.

Your people skills are not only measured by how you navigate those relationships but also by how you manage the people who cause pain. Every business leader experiences *people pains*. That is normal when dealing with people. And business is all about people. You have staff, employees, clients and customers; some of whom are really difficult. The purpose of this book is to give you practical and timely tools to navigate them and fix the people pains in your organization.

CHAPTER 1

IT ALL BEGINS WITH THE LEADER

Several years ago, I went to work for an organization with a dysfunctional team. While most of the team members were skilled in their respective roles, the staff dynamics needed some real work. There was a lack of trust within the team, as well as low morale, conflict and low motivation.

A part of my job description included serving as the chief of staff. I was responsible for managing staff members, supervising them and developing them. My big goal was to improve staff morale and change the staff culture. I put some things in place, such as organizing team socials outside of work, celebrating wins, affirming the team for positive behaviors, and facilitating learning opportunities with a view to begin shifting the culture.

I ran into challenges because the senior leader did not value what I was trying to do. He did not value the team. He viewed the team members as "work horses" who were there to accomplish what *he* wanted. He did not fully embrace and support my efforts. As a result, the culture of our team continued to erode. Not only did he refuse to support my efforts, he promoted and created drama around the office.

Even though I knew how to build a healthy team, my efforts needed the senior leader's buy-in, which I did not have. He needed to model positive values and help me create structures that would improve the culture and morale. I spent the next several years watching high turnover on the staff, resolving conflict between employees, dealing with performance issues, managing negativity and dealing with low morale. It was a difficult position for me and very frustrating to say the least.

I share this experience, not to be critical of that leader, but to illustrate a lesson. The lesson being, if you are the leader of your organization, reducing drama and building a healthy culture begins with YOU! Leaders are the curators of culture. Leaders set the vision for organizations, but most importantly, leaders set the culture. A healthy work environment begins with the *leader*.

My amazing mother-in-law, Barbara Johnson, who recently passed away from her battle with cancer, had some great sayings. She always said that the fish rots from the head. From a biological standpoint, I do not know if that is true. But from a leadership perspective, it's spot on. If there is dysfunction, negativity and drama in the workplace, the leader is generally responsible for it.

It may be that the leader directly contributes to the drama and negative culture by his or her behaviors, like the leader mentioned above. It could also be due to the leader not doing anything to address it. When leaders allow dysfunctional behaviors to continue, he or she is part of the problem because leaders have the responsibility of setting a positive workplace culture.

Model Desired Behaviors

A big part of setting a positive workplace culture is to model the behaviors that you want to see in your organization. People do as people see. Your employees are watching you. When you do not exhibit positive behaviors, you are giving them permission to do the same.

I believe that one of the most important traits for leading a group of people is to show compassion. If you demonstrate compassion for them, they will demonstrate compassion for each other. How do you show compassion for your employees? One way is to show kindness, respect, understanding and grace.

Another way is to make them feel valued by praising them and rewarding them for their work. When an employee does something well, they need to be praised. Many leaders undervalue this approach. They see work only as a contract. In other words, you do the work and you get a salary and benefits in return. The truth of the matter is most employees need more than that. They *deserve* more than that. Your employees want to feel valued and cared for.

Many leaders are all about criticizing and correcting their employees. Accountability is an essential value in the workplace. If employees are underperforming or behaving inappropriately, then that needs to be addressed. This is not the only time your employees need to hear from you. They need to be recognized for a job well done.

Praising employees needs to be honest and authentic. They know when you are pouring on the syrup in an effort to manipulate. One of the ways to add value to your employees is not only by praising them for their hard work, but highlighting their positive personal qualities. This demonstrates that you appreciate them for not only what they do, but who they are.

How do you reward employees? Get to know your staff. Each of them has his or her unique personality. You have to learn what motivates each person. Some employees are motivated by verbal affirmation. They love to be bragged on. Others appreciate and value tangible rewards, such as an extra day off, a bonus, a raise or some other visible reward. This shows that you care about them.

Reinforce Healthy Values

If you walk into the lobby of most businesses, you may notice a frame on the wall with the company's mission statement, vision statement and a list of values. These statements are important. They provide insight into that company in regards to its direction and purpose. Values can be a bit tricky because there are different types of values. Values are the deep beliefs of an organization that describe and define what is most important to them. A few examples could be excellence, integrity, compassion, dedication and service. There are hundreds. Values not only define what is important, but they should drive behavior. They set the norms for how employees are to behave with each other and with your customers.

Some values are aspirational. They describe what the organization is striving to be. That is fine as long as you are intentional about moving the organization in that direction. Values can also be espoused or operational. When I observe organizational values on the wall when I walk into businesses, I will often ask some of the employees to tell me about their values. Often, I am told that they are only words and that they do not reflect the real behavior around the office; these are otherwise known as espoused or stated values.

Operational values are the ones that are really being lived out in the workplace. All organizations operate by values whether or not they even recognize it. Your real values are what you actually live and express. Your values may not even be the ones that are written in the frame on the wall. Your real values are how you and your employees are truly demonstrating.

If you are the senior leader of an organization, a leader of a team or the leader of a department, I want to encourage you to work with your group to discern your real values. After you accomplish that important step, then you need to embed them into the group. You do that by modeling the values, keeping the values before your employees by discussing them, complimenting employees when they demonstrate them and confronting employees when they violate them.

It is important to evaluate these values periodically. In your team meetings, devote time to ask team members how they are doing in regards to living out the company's values. Have some discussions around that theme and constantly evaluate them with your team. I also suggest including your values in your annual performance evaluation process.

Most performance reviews only deal with how people are doing with accomplishing the tasks and responsibilities of their jobs. There needs to be evaluation of how they are behaving in the organization as well. This is how you reinforce your values.

Make the Right Hires

I have a great business friend who often says that we should hire and fire based on our organizational values. Maintaining a healthy culture involves conditioning your current employees to behave in a way that's consistent with the organizational values. The one thing that can disrupt your culture is who comes in next. When you are making new hires, don't just look at their experience, education, success in other jobs and background; build some interview questions around your value system to make sure that this person will be the right fit for your organization. Don't forget to include this when you are talking to their references. Most people know how to interview with a prospective employer; they know what to say and how to say it. So, you will want to talk to their current and former bosses and work colleagues to make sure that they have a history of living out the values that you have established.

In his popular bestseller, Good to Great, author Jim Collins considers getting the right people in the right seats on the bus. The bus is your organization and the seats represent the various positions. Hiring the right people is not only determined by skills, experience and background, but specific character qualities. I have seen many highly skilled people who are sharp in their performance, but they are also negative and toxic. These are not the kind of people you want on your bus. As a leader, you must hire people who will help you build and maintain a healthy culture in your workplace.

It only takes a few people to break down your culture. If you lead a small organization, just one person can disrupt your culture. Stay on top of it by bringing in the right people who reflect your organizational values. Keep in mind, there is no perfect culture. All of us are imperfect people. When people work in groups, there will be issues. At times, there will even be personality differences, disagreements and conflict. As a leader, you must be proactive in addressing culture issues the moment they emerge. Don't let them linger. It will only get worse and begin eroding your organization's relational system.

As a kid, I played baseball all the way through high school. I am still a huge baseball fan. Sorry Dodgers fans, but I am an Angels fan. I was really sad when Joe Maddon was released as the manager. Before becoming the manager for the Angels, he managed the Chicago Cubs from 2015 through 2019. Can I make my National League friends angry by saying the Cubs are my favorite National League Team? When they won the 2016 World Series, I was ecstatic. I could not believe it. They finally ended the 108-year World Series drought. Do you want to know why they were the champions in 2016? Obviously, they had some amazing players including Kris Bryant, Javier Baez, Anthony Rizzo, Ben Zobrist and Kyle Hendricks. The skill level of the players was extremely high and they worked well together. They were excellent at their craft and their respective positions. The other reason they had a successful year was because Joe Maddon had curated a winning culture. He not only developed a strong team through trades and bringing up future stars from the minors, he created a positive culture. Maddon was a leader. He understood the psychology of building a healthy and winning team. He knew how to motivate his players.

The same is true in business. In order to have a successful business, the senior leader has to curate a positive culture and environment for his or her workplace team. That responsibility is on you as the leader. By being proactive, you can minimize drama and relational conflict in the workplace.

CHAPTER 2

MANAGING DIFFICULT PERSONALITIES

In one of the organizations where I served as the senior leader, I had a board member who did not like me. *How do I know that?* Well, he told me so. Gotta love his honesty though. He made leadership miserable for me. He always found some reason to be critical of me; I couldn't do anything right in his eyes. I dreaded our monthly board meetings because I knew I was going to face his criticism and disapproval of my leadership.

My stomach was literally in knots a day or two prior to our meetings. This went on for *months*. I have always felt that I was good at working with different kinds of people and I have learned to win over people who were critical of me in leadership roles. But I met my challenge with this guy. I decided to take him to lunch. One of my fundamental beliefs is if someone does not like you, often that is because they do not know you.

My strategy was to treat him to a nice lunch, ask questions to learn more about him and give him an opportunity to see my heart. You're not going to believe this, but that is when he shared with me that he did not care for me and that he did not vote for me to lead the organization. Just what you want to hear when you're spending hard-earned money to treat someone to lunch.

I left that lunch thinking I had started my leadership with absolutely no credibility with him, and it was going to be difficult to cultivate and build up that credibility. He continued to criticize me personally, to others behind my back and in front of the other board members at our monthly board meetings.

A few months later, I had had enough. As expected, I walked into the monthly board meeting and he started with his negative talk about me; this time, the issue was related to a specific incident that had gone wrong but wasn't my fault. Still, he assigned the blame to me. He faulted me because it had happened on my watch. I did not handle it very well. My anger and frustration rose to a level that caused me to say some things I later regretted. I stormed out of the meeting– *a big mistake.*

My actions and words shocked the other board members. In fact, I lost leadership capital with some of them and I had to work to rebuild their trust and credibility over the next few months, which I did. I did apologize to him and to the entire board, but the damage was already done. That was a leadership mistake on my part. I did not use emotional intelligence skills. I allowed my emotions to take over. My emotional brain hijacked my rational brain and I sabotaged my leadership in that quick moment. This was a learning and growing moment for me. I realized that if I am going to survive the crucible of leadership, I would need to master some skills for managing difficult people.

Leadership involves working with difficult people. Management is an important part of leadership. Management is more than managing projects, strategies, systems and processes. Management involves managing *people*. In fact, this is the most important aspect of management.

Emotional intelligence is a key skill needed for management and leadership. Good leaders keep their emotions in check when dealing with difficult personalities. Not only do you need to control your emotions, you have to control the emotions of others. That does not mean you have control over their feelings and actions. It means that you do not allow their emotional reactions to control *your* responses. You have to remain controlled and professional, otherwise you will lose leadership credibility.

If you are leading an organization, you'll have different types of personalities represented in your business. You have to learn to manage them. If you learn how to lead different personalities, you will be successful as a leader. Let's address three personality types that can sabotage your leadership and disrupt the proper functioning of your team and organization.

The Narcissist

In Greek mythology, Narcissus was a hunter who found himself to be so beautiful that he became fixated by his own reflection in a pool. His fixation was so strong, he lost the will to do anything else, and he died as a result of it. The story of Narcissus inspired the name for a personality disorder known as narcissism.

Narcissists tend to have an exaggerated sense of self-importance. Narcissists have a negative impact on those around them and can even destroy the people who are around them. This is problematic in business. In business, it is important to have team players. Narcissists are not team players because they only care about themselves and their own agenda.

Narcissists lack empathy. Most of us are able to understand how others are feeling. Not only are narcissists unable to understand how others are feeling, they have no desire to understand. They are inherently selfish people.

If you are a competent leader, you will be committed to building collaborative, cohesive teams. Narcissists, if they are not managed, will destroy your efforts in building cohesive teams that carry out the mission of your organization.

Narcissists tend to dominate conversations. They want conversations to revolve around them, their needs and their agenda. They do not listen to other people. If you have narcissists on your team, you will have a major challenge in meetings when collaborating over strategy and decision-making. Narcissists do not listen to the ideas of others, but insist on being heard.

When teams collaborate over issues within the business, it is important to have team players who bring good ideas, but are also open to the ideas of others. This is how you arrive at good decisions and direction for the organization. Narcissists disrupt this process, because they interrupt others when they are talking. Narcissists can also cause others in the group to emotionally shut down. When you have a few people on your team, or even one person, who constantly shoots down the ideas of others, they will become silent. Even though they have great ideas, they will keep them to themselves and you will never hear the great ideas that others have. As a leader, you have to manage these people so that everyone has the opportunity to share their ideas.

Narcissists feel that they are the most important person in the room and the smartest person in the room. They assume that their contribution is vital and that the rest of the group cannot manage or operate without them. They also have a sense of entitlement. In other words, they feel they deserve special attention and treatment. Nothing breaks down the work of organizational teams like narcissists.

Narcissists do not follow the rules. In fact, they believe they are *above* the rules. In other words, the rules do not apply to them. Rules are for *other* team members to abide by– not them.

Narcissists are manipulative. They are deceptive because they can be charming, especially if it suits their cause. They can come across as friendly, considerate and endearing just to get their way. But the motive is not genuine. They use charm and manipulation to get their way. A good leader will be able to see through this and not allow that person to control and manipulate the group. Narcissists will manipulate people's thoughts and emotions in an attempt to influence them with the sole purpose of benefiting themselves. They love working under weak leaders because a weak leader will not be able to see through them and manage their manipulative behaviors.

In my work, I have the opportunity to watch team dynamics. It is amusing to watch a person – not the leader – who is able to control the meetings. Often, it is the narcissist who plays this role. Narcissists like to control people and decisions. They want things to go their way.

Narcissists do not accept responsibility. They play the "blame game." They take the credit when things go well, but assign blame to others when things do not go well. They do not receive criticism and constructive feedback very well because they not only have a sense of self-importance, but a sense of perfection. They could never do anything wrong.

Maybe you are a leader with a few narcissists on your team or staff, who are disrupting the effective dynamics of your group. If you do not manage them, they will create dysfunction on your team. The good news is they can be managed, but you have to know how to do it.

Educate yourself. Learn as much as you can about them. The narcissistic disorder is something many counselors deal with every day. If you have a counselor friend, speak to them about the disorder and get some feedback on how to manage these people in the workplace. Learn their strengths and weaknesses. And then learn how to leverage their strengths and manage their weaknesses.

It is also important to create boundaries and be very clear and direct about those boundaries. As a senior leader in several organizations, I have had to deal with narcissistic personalities. One technique I have used is creating meeting norms. For example, I always made a point to take ideas from everyone. And when someone is talking, do not interrupt. Hear them out and be open-minded to what they are saying. Continue to stress to your team members that this is a group effort and it's important to hear from everyone in the room.

As a leader, you have to be very assertive with this personality type. Boundaries are like fences. Fences, at times, need to be reinforced. With the narcissist, you have to be consistent and assertive in reinforcing the boundaries, norms and expectations, otherwise they will take over the group. You cannot afford for this to happen.

The Dramatizer

You want positive energy in the workplace. While drama is a type of energy, it's certainly not what you want in the workplace. The dramatizer brings a lot of energy, but it's often negative and unproductive. Of course, drama in the workplace is inevitable because we are working with people. Humans are emotional beings. We all feel and express emotions—but dramatizers do it in ways that create bad energy.

The dramatizer turns the focus off of the main objective of your business. They like to stir the pot by gossiping and making a big deal out of anything and everything. After a while, your employees become solely focused on the drama rather than the mission, vision and strategies of your business.

Workplace drama takes the form of gossip, rumors, complaints and office conflict. The dramatizer elevates the conflict, rather than reducing the conflict. In fact, the dramatizer stirs the pot so that the drama continues and grows in intensity. They *thrive* on drama. In fact, if there is no drama, they are not happy. They get an adrenaline rush from it.

Drama is a destructive force in organizations. As a leader, you have to be able to detect it. Office drama is not always loud and visible. Sometimes, it is very quiet and subtle. Some dramatizers work behind the scenes by going to different offices, spreading rumors and gossip. Dramatizers are good at creating division and coalitions that support their cause. A good leader has to be able to spot this type of drama so it can be dealt with immediately.

As a leader, how do you deal with the dramatizers? Keep in mind that they are acting out for attention. When they begin to complain to you, don't feed it. Acknowledge them and say, "I'm sorry you feel that way" and then move on. What they are looking for is attention and for you to feed it. *Don't do that.* You will only elevate it and make it worse.

As a leader, other concerned people in your office may approach you with concerns about the dramatizer. Encourage them to respond the same way. Acknowledge them, but move on. Don't give them the attention they are seeking.

You, as the leader, have to set boundaries with them. You also need to be assertive and confrontational at times. Their behaviors are childlike and you have to be direct with them just like you do with children. Teachers are good at this because they are trained to deal with this kind of behavior. With children, you have to set expectations, be direct and put consequences in place. You cannot allow the dramatizers to erode the positive culture you are trying to build within your organization.

The Troublemaker

This person likes to disagree for the sake of disagreement. They thrive on it. Like the dramatizer, they do it because they want attention. They can make the workplace a miserable place for you and for your employees. They create unpleasantness, quarrels and conflict.

The way this person will create issues for you is defiance for authority. They question you and criticize your leadership. Good leaders do need to be open to criticism, feedback and allow others to disagree. That can be very helpful to you as a leader. With the troublemaker, it is different. The troublemaker is not giving you feedback because he or she is concerned about the organization and wants what is best, they are doing it for the sake of disagreeing.

Communication skills are crucial in dealing with the troublemaker. Accountability is also key. You have to let the troublemaker know that his or her behavior is unacceptable and will not be tolerated. One of the reasons that a company's culture can become unhealthy is by allowing this kind of behavior to continue. Many leaders choose to avoid these people and their behavior because it is hard confronting this kind of person, but you must do it. Your company's health depends on your taking the right action.

I have always recognized the people who fit this category. In order to keep them from disrupting the progress in meetings, often I will sit with them prior to the meetings to go over the agenda and ask them how they feel about it. Troublemakers look for venues to express their disagreements. If you do not create spaces for them to do it, they will create their own spaces. Often, the spaces they choose are not the right place or context.

I encourage you to do the same. Set a time to meet with them. Explain your decisions, positions and proposals and give them an opportunity to share their opinions. I have found that this often shuts them down when you meet with the entire group because they have already had a space or venue for airing their opinions. Again, setting values, norms and expectations are important for managing this personality.

There are other personality types, but the three that I have mentioned are the primary difficult personalities. As a leader, stay calm, communicate clearly, set boundaries and confront as often as you need to with difficult personalities in your organization.

CHAPTER 3

TURNING CONFLICT INTO CREATIVITY

One of my closest friends has been a business owner for most of his professional life. He called me one day and shared that there was intense conflict within his office. He had a staff of 50, and things were not going well. He told me he did not know how to resolve it and asked if I could come in and work with him and his team to resolve it, and set up a system for navigating conflict in the future.

I agreed, and wrote a proposal for how I would address it. He signed off and I went to work. I spent about three months analyzing the situation through observation, confidential questionnaires and employee interviews. Before I started the project, he shared with me that the conflict was so emotional and intense, two of his employees almost got into a literal fist fight in the parking lot. When he told me that, I considered ripping up the contract and returning his deposit. *Do I need to bring a couple pairs of Everlast boxing gloves and let them just go at it?*, I wondered.

Fast forwarding, the outcomes were positive. We resolved the immediate problems, set up some conflict resolution measures, and some hard decisions were made to rebuild the culture. Some of the actions required hard decisions, including resignations and terminations.

This situation escalated because it was an unchecked conflict. It had been allowed to go on for way too long. Many business leaders do not want to deal with conflict. They think that, if they just give it time, the conflict will ride away into the sunset. Unfortunately, unchecked conflict only gets worse.

The reason this chapter is so important is because leaders lack two important resources for managing conflict. I call them the "Two T's." The first is *time*. As a business leader, you are so busy running your company, you simply do not have the time to address and resolve conflict when it emerges. Oftentimes, you may not even be aware of conflict because you are swamped with the responsibilities of running the business.

The second is *training*. Business leaders know their products and services and how to run a business, but they are not experts at resolving and utilizing conflict so that creativity and productivity grow from it.

Understanding Conflict Is Normal

We tend to incorrectly define conflict. Often viewed as abnormal or unnatural, the truth is that conflict is very normal. From marriage and parenting to friends and colleagues, we deal with relationships each and every day. With these relationships can come conflict. The business culture is a social context as well; if you are in relationships with others, regardless of the context, there will be conflict.

The workplace is a breeding ground for conflict because it is an environment in which people with different personalities, communication styles, and worldviews intersect and interact. The work environment is naturally a place of stress and tension due to various expectations, obligations and deadlines. Work can be quite demanding and difficult.

Conflict occurs in the workplace because decisions have to be made. Often, work teams do not find complete agreement when thinking of solutions, solving problems and making decisions. Everyone has an opinion about how to do work. The problem comes when we are married to our ideas and opinions, refusing to listen to the views of others on the team. This creates tension– but you must understand that this is normal. We do not have to always agree with each other when working together. It is the sharing of various ideas and viewpoints that lead to the best solutions. The problem is when we are dogmatic and stubborn in our positions. Often, we are insistent on getting our way rather than working for what is best for the company.

Speed Leas is an author who has done extensive work on the subject of conflict and he talks about the five levels of conflict. When resolving conflict, it is important to note that not all conflicts exist at the same level. To resolve it, you have to know what level you're working with.

Level 1 is the basic level. This is where we always are. There is no level 0. Level one is the position that we are always in because we are all different and see the world differently. Level one is simply a problem to be solved. When you walk into a boardroom or conference room and the presider details a situation that requires a decision and asks for ideas for solutions, this places you in a level one conflict.

At this level, everyone is focused on the problem and finding solutions. At this point, it is not emotional. The natural thing will be for everyone in the room to respond by sharing ideas for solving the problem at hand. It is at this point you will observe that everyone has a different perspective. This is a good place to be, especially if everyone is focused on the problem and coming up with a solution that will solve the problem.

This type of discussion, if managed well, can bring creative and wise solutions.

Level 2 is what Leas calls the disagreement stage. Level two becomes more intense as you begin to see emotional ownership of ideas. At this stage, you have to be careful about becoming too dogmatic about your perspective. Even though you have strong feelings about your viewpoint, you still need to be open to the other ideas being presented. This is still a good place to be because the focus is still on the problem. Everyone wants to find the right solution.

Level 3 moves you close to the "red zone." This is called the contest. At this stage, the emotional intensity grows and people begin to lose sight of the problem. Levels 1 and 2 are the win-win stages. Everyone is focused on solving the problem and coming up with a solution that everyone can live with. Level three causes employees to see their fellow workers as competitors; the goal now is to be right and win the argument. What is best for the company no longer matters.

Level 4 moves you into the "red zone" or danger zone. All perspective is lost now. It is highly emotional with battle language. The issue is no longer the problem to be solved; your fellow colleagues are now the issue. The conflict becomes very personal. At this level, it is difficult to solve the problem.

Level 5 is World War III. It is intractable. The situation is way out of hand. People at this level are completely emotional and irrational, viewing their fellow colleagues as adversaries. People who once worked well together are now polarized and relationships are broken.

As a leader in your organization, you have to know what level a specific conflict is in. This is important because you have the role to bring it down. For example, if you sense that a conflict is at a level 2, you will need to bring it down to a level 1.

How does a leader navigate conflict between individuals and teams? It is important to remind your employees of the value of respecting each other. This means respecting another opinion— whether you agree or not. You also have to remind your employees that the larger organization is more important than any single individual in the company.

As a senior leader presiding over meetings, I have found myself in this situation many times. One practice that I have always used is what I call the "pause." I will shut down the meeting temporarily and ask those in the meeting to take a break of 15-30 minutes and then come back to the issue. This gives people time to bring their emotions down and to think rationally about the issue or problem at hand. When they return to the room, I will emphasize to the group the need for coming up with a solution that is best for the company, no matter whose idea it is.

I have found great success in this practice because people do not think clearly and logically when they are emotional. As a leader, you are the emotional guide of your group. You not only manage processes and decisions, you manage *emotions*.

Your Employees Have Different Conflict Styles

All of us have a unique conflict style. And most people do not like conflict. It is very uncomfortable. Keep in mind that if you are a leader or an employee in an organization, you are going to deal with conflict with your fellow colleagues. It is important to understand your style and the styles of your colleagues. This will be helpful in solving conflict.

Some people are confrontational. These professional bullies use force and manipulation to get what they want. Often, their preferences are not well-thought-out or even best for the company. They get their way because they are loud and people give in to them because they just want to be done with the issue. As a leader, you have to remind this person that the issue is an organizational one and it is important to hear, listen to and consider the input of others; you must be assertive with that person.

Some of your employees are accommodating. They give in easily. They will share their opinions and viewpoints, but will shut down when bullied by a person with a more confrontational style. As a leader, you must add value to that person's ideas and encourage them to speak. They will share their ideas, but they will not provide rationale when shut down by a bully. If you do not encourage them to continue speaking, you will miss some good rationales. Again, they will share their ideas but will not share their reasons when they sense that they are not being heard.

Others are avoiding. These are the types who despise conflict. In fact, they absolutely hate conflict. In emotional and intense meetings, their goal is not to come to a consensus that is the best solution, but rather come to a decision (any decision) so the conflict ends. They are not always shy and reserved. They simply shrink back because they do not want to be a part of the dynamics in the room. As their leader, you have to ask for their input and assure them that there is psychological safety in sharing their input. Give them the assurance that you want to hear what they have to say. That will help them to feel comfortable in spite of the fact that someone else may shoot down what they have to say.

You also have your collaborators. These individuals are your secret sauce. These are the people who are bold enough to share, kind enough to listen to others who are not being so kind and strong enough to face resistance. These individuals are good at keeping the focus on the issues and evaluating the pros and cons of every idea presented. You want to capitalize on the skills of these individuals.

Use Conflict as a Collaborative Resource

Not only is conflict natural, but it is necessary in business and organizations. It is through conflict, if managed properly, that the best ideas for solutions emerge. Learn how to utilize conflict so that it is productive and leads to creativity.

Conflict, in and of itself, is not bad, unhealthy or abnormal. Conflict is unhealthy only when it becomes toxic. Conflict is dysfunctional when it is not managed well. When managed well, conflict is the best way to find solutions for solving problems and making decisions.

Dr. David Augsburger was one of my doctoral professors and I had the privilege of taking a course he taught on conflict management. In conflict, there is "my way" and "your way." But Dr. Augsburger introduced a "third way." Often, conflict is not philosophical or principle-centered. It is "method"-centered. In other words, there are strong disagreements about how to do something. There are a million different ways to do something and most of them can be right. In conflict, we are often married to our method and we are closed-minded about other methods or ideas.

The "third way" concept means that when two people or work groups come to an impasse, both parties should abandon their perspective or ideas and collaborate together to come up with a solution that works for both parties. I can tell you that every time I have used this concept, the solution we arrived at was much better than any of the ideas we were previously sold on.

As a leader, instill the value of collaboration within your organization. Model it by practicing the "third way" when you differ with another employee. Show them how it works. Create a culture of listening and respect. All conflict is negotiable. If it cannot be resolved, then utilize conflict to develop the best ideas for solving issues and making decisions in your organization.

CHAPTER 4

DEALING WITH APATHY AND LOW MOTIVATION

In one of my management roles, I had the privilege of supervising a sharp, bright employee with great potential– but he had lost his motivation. We had a very good relationship and enjoyed meeting together, planning together and celebrating his successes on the job.

But something had happened! He became *apathetic*. So, I did what any supervisor would do. I had conversations with him, provided support and accountability to elevate motivation, and reinforced expectations. I realized my approach was not working; none of the traditional methods helped.

In one of our weekly one-on-one meetings, he became very transparent with me and indicated that his salary was very low for the work we were asking him to do. He had not received a raise in a few years. Again, I did what any manager should do. I listened to him and followed up on that conversation by conducting a compensation study. The results were embarrassing. He was definitely underpaid.

This was affecting his motivation level because he did not feel that the organization was being fair or even cared for him. I was able to get a salary increase approved. He was so appreciative and the quality of his work improved.

I think the salary increase was only a small part of the solution. What impacted him the most was the fact that I listened to him and brought the situation to the senior leadership and board and advocated for him to get the raise he deserved. He felt like he had been heard, was valued and cared for by the actions that I took.

Let me ask you Do you have employees who come in late, leave early, call in sick often, don't meet deadlines and seem disengaged? You are not alone. Employees from all industries and companies feel this way. One of the biggest problems with disengaged employees is absenteeism. Absenteeism can cost a company $2,660 per year, per salaried employee.

Many are talking about the "Great Resignation." Millions of people across the nation are quitting their jobs. A part of it has to do with low salary and benefits. The vast majority of people are leaving their jobs because they do not feel valued. Some sociologists and economists call this the "Great Re-evaluation." People are not just looking at their salary and benefits, they are asking the internal question *Does my employer truly care about me?*

As a business leader, learn what motivates your employees. They will be more loyal and more productive. Recently, I have consulted with a number of employers who are struggling to keep their employees. Knowing what motivates your employees and meeting their needs will greatly increase your employee retention. In the long run, your company is going to be healthier and stronger when you value and take care of your employees.

Care For Your Employees

Leadership seems to be a big buzz word in the business world today. There are many discussions around what makes a person a good leader. A great vision caster, a strategic thinker, an executioner; these are all important traits in a good leader. I believe the most important traits and characteristics have to do with the soft skills of leadership. Empathy, in our day and time, is what is most needed from leaders. Employees who feel cared for are 71% less likely to experience burnout in their jobs.

Herb Kelleher, the founder of Southwest Airlines, was a leader I admired and respected because he focused on the soft skills of leadership. He had a non-traditional business plan for starting an airline, but it worked. It is said that he was the most transformative figure and character in the history of modern aviation. He was brilliant, strategic and had a courageous entrepreneurial spirit.

What set Herb apart from many CEO's was the fact that he had amazing emotional intelligence skills and empathy. He truly valued and cared for his employees. Herb empathized with his employees. He supported them in their failures and grief. He celebrated their successes and victories. He showed them how much he admired, valued and loved them as people, not just workers. Many employers see their people only as hired servants; not people. Herb took a personal interest in his employees and once said, "Your best customers are your employees."

Many leaders get caught up in their titles and positions, creating a stark separation from their employees. Your employees want to be connected to you and want something from you emotionally. Trust me - you will not lose leadership credibility by being caring, empathetic and authentic. In fact, you will gain influence by establishing an emotional connection with your employees.

Show your employees you care about them. When they are having a bad day or dealing with a challenging life situation, demonstrate compassion. When they achieve success, let them know how proud you are of them. Get to know your employees. Ask them about their lives. Get to know the names of their spouses, children and some personal things about them. This will go a long way in their motivation. When they know that you care about them, they will be loyal to you and the company and will be motivated and productive.

Maybe you're thinking and saying, "So, Reggie, I am not into this soft skill and touchy-feely stuff. What's the benefit to me and my business?" Well, rather than listening to me, how about listening to statistics?

Research shows 85% of employees are not engaged at work. This is a major problem in the workforce. Engaged employees are 87% less likely to resign. Currently, 81% are thinking about quitting for a better job. A recent Gallup Poll indicates that only 15% of employees feel engaged. More than $450 billion is lost each year due to unmotivated employees. Studies show that companies with the best corporate culture increased revenue by 68%.

So, I can tell you the benefits. You are going to keep most of your employees. They are going to be happier, and as a result be more productive. Based on the research, the bottom line is going to be more financially beneficial. One study found that the average cost of losing a good employee costs companies $29,000 a year.

One more point about caring for your employees - be concerned about their life-work balance. Encourage your employees to take care of themselves. Mitigate working at nights after hours and on weekends. Encourage them to spend time with family and friends, exercise and engage in some of their hobbies and passions. Many employees are on the verge of burnout because the demands of their jobs are too much. Give them adequate time off for vacations and recovery time. By doing so, they are going to be so much more fresh for the job while on the job.

Now, I want to address another push back you may have. Focusing on the soft skills of leadership, leading with empathy and caring for your employees does not mean that there is no accountability. You still need to set high standards, have expectations and confront when an employee is not meeting the standards. Trust me on this one - when you do have to confront them, it will be better received because they know that you have their best interest at heart and that you care about them personally and professionally.

Reward Your Employees

I often chuckle inside when I hear leaders of organizations say, "well, I pay them well and provide benefits. What more do they want?" Well, the truth of the matter is they do want more. This is not an issue of entitlement on their part. It is human nature to want to be appreciated for contributions. Whether you like it or not, you need to reward your employees. This will look different for each of your employees.

There are two types of motivation. There is *achievement* motivation and *reward* motivation. You have some employees who are motivated by achievement. That's me. I am a highly motivated individual with initiative and I am motivated by simply accomplishing tasks. My joy and satisfaction comes from accomplishing tasks and doing them with excellence.

How do you motivate these individuals? William Schutz published The Human Element in 1994 in which he talked about psychic pay. People who are motivated by achievement are not necessarily motivated by money. They are motivated by having their emotional needs met on the job.

They have a need for inclusion, which is the feeling of belonging to the organization. This satisfies their need for feeling significant. They have a need for control. This satisfies their need that they are contributing and are competent. They have a need for affection. They want to know that they are cared for and have worth. *How do you motivate these individuals?* You tell them. You let them know they are significant, competent and bring worth to the organization. They want to know that you recognize their achievements.

Verbal affirmation of their accomplishments will motivate them and create a sense of loyalty to you and your organization.

You have some employees who are motivated by tangible rewards. In other words, they are motivated by external factors such as raises, bonuses and promotions. They are motivated by incentives and reinforcement. Job security, recognition and professional development are important to these kinds of employees. They also enjoy public praise. Learn to compliment your employees both privately and publicly. In private, they will know you mean it because it is a personal and private conversation. In public, they will feel a sense of pride because you are elevating them before their colleagues.

Learn What Motivates Your Employees

I can't stress this enough, but it's so important to get to know your employees. *How do you do that?* Spend time with them. Some of your employees are motivated *intrinsically*, meaning they gain motivation by achieving tasks and hearing words of affirmation and appreciation. Others are motivated *extrinsically*, meaning they are motivated by tangible factors.

When you spend one-on-one time with your employees, it demonstrates that you care. You will also have an opportunity to get to know them and learn what motivates them. You will learn important things about their personalities, what they are passionate about and what drives them. Knowing what drives them will help you to become a better manager.

If you have great employees, don't assume that you can always count on them being highly motivated. As the leader, it is your job and responsibility to meet their emotional needs so that they remain highly motivated and competent.

If you have some employees who are performing at a sub-par level and they have low motivation, change your approach. Begin to demonstrate care and compassion by giving verbal affirmations and rewards. When employees' emotional needs are not being met, they will experience anger or apathy. They will feel anger because they feel that you do not care about them, their needs or their contributions. Others will become apathetic and simply check out. They will be at work, but you will not get their best.

CHAPTER 5

NAVIGATING PERFORMANCE ISSUES

At another company where I held a senior leadership position, we hired a young man; it would be his first job working in the industry. He made a lot of mistakes, mostly with people. He lacked specific skills needed, but I was confident he could develop them.

This was early in my leadership career, so I took more traditional and punitive approaches to correcting these kinds of issues. I addressed these issues in our check-in meetings and performance evaluations. I did not see the needle moving in the right direction, so I made the decision to terminate him. Before I pulled the plug, I shared it with my wife who begged me not to do it.

On the Myers-Briggs Personality Indicator Test, I am a thinker (T). I tend to make decisions based on what is rational and logical. My rational brain said he is not doing the job well, so he needs to be terminated.

My wife, on the other hand, is a feeler (F). By her way of thinking, she felt this decision would devastate this employee; he had a young family he had to provide for. Well, my wife, as she normally does, got to me. She turned me into a soft feeler in this situation, so I decided to keep him. I decided to spend more time coaching him in his role. I turned our weekly check-in meetings into coaching sessions, where I taught him leadership lessons and we worked on his people skills.

I also invited him to sit in on meetings he normally would not attend to watch me model positive leadership behaviors. To fast forward, he was open, teachable and humble. Not only did he eventually succeed in this position, today he is an effective leader and has experienced success in his career.

I am so happy that I did not follow my initial impulse for two reasons. One was for the good of this person. He grew, developed and excelled. Second, I learned a valuable lesson. Sometimes, performance issues are not because a person is lazy or has a bad attitude. They simply need someone to invest in them. This is a lesson I have continued to employ in my leadership of people, especially with performance issues.

What executive or manager doesn't have problems with employees who do not meet expectations, perform well and produce the desired results? Maybe you are reading this and, lately, you have been losing sleep over performance issues in your business. If so, you are not alone and this chapter is for you!

Hire the Right People

We talked about this in chapter 1, but I want to get a bit more specific and practical. Begin with your corporate values. It is important for organizations to set values that involve initiative, responsibility, effort and excellence. Again, you have to get the right people on the bus.

This part of the chapter does not necessarily address the current issues you are having with some of your employees. My intention here is to be proactive and futuristic; as you make future hires, you will make good decisions.

This begins with your hiring process. Focus on character. Initiative, responsibility, effort and excellence are values that are a part of a person's character. Too often, we look only at education, training, skills and experience. Don't get me wrong, these things are extremely important, but don't forget character. As you interview prospective employees, ask them about their values and then ask how they live them out in the workplace. People will often know the right answers to give during interviews, but asking the right questions will provide you with insight into their character.

One of the techniques I use is to ask situational questions when interviewing. I will create a situation and ask them to tell me how they would handle the situation. Taking the time to run references and asking the right questions goes a long way. We often rush through this part of the interview process and we miss important details about a prospective employee. Take your time and ask many questions. More importantly, ask deep questions, both of the prospective employee and of his or her references.

Make Your Expectations Clear

Now, let's get into your current problem. You have employees who are incompetent and underperforming. You are pulling your hair out. You are not sleeping at night. You are frustrated and you simply do not know what to do.

The first thing you must do is have an honest conversation with that person. Use the "sandwich approach." Start with positive things with that particular employee by complimenting specific things about who they are, what they have accomplished and the potential you see in them. Leaders often get emotional, critical and reprimanding. If you begin this conversation by complimenting the person, the second part of the sandwich will go much more smoothly. The second part of the conversation is the confrontation. That sounds like a negative word, doesn't it? I don't mean it negatively. It simply means that you have an honest conversation with that person about meeting expectations, not meeting deadlines and not producing.

You already know this, but make sure that you document this conversation and place it in their employee file for the records. Close the conversation with the third part of the sandwich approach by affirming that person. Let them know that you believe in them and that you believe they can succeed. Let them know that you want them to succeed and that the company needs for them to succeed.

Another approach I often take is I will ask them if there is anything going on in their personal lives that may be affecting their performance. This is where your emotional intelligence skills are needed. I have worked with people whose performance was low and it was because they were dealing with something personally. This is why you want to learn as much about what is going on with that person as possible. If they are dealing with personal issues, then you can offer to help them and make some concessions.

Maybe they need some time off to deal with their personal situation.

What happens if their performance does not improve? You will need to put them on an Performance Improvement Plan or an Employee Improvement Plan. This needs to be in writing and it needs to be very specific, detailing your expectations. There needs to be tangible and measurable indicators that will mark improvement in their performance.

This involves writing a plan and meeting with the employee to go over it. Again, that meeting needs to be documented. People have different ideas about the timeline of Performance Improvement Plans. I recommend three months. This demonstrates that you are making the effort to help the employee succeed. It also gives the employee enough time to meet the goals of the plan.

Let me share a word of caution. Do not wait until the annual review to address performance issues. There are problems with doing that. One, the employee will rightfully ask why you waited so long. I have made this mistake and I was like a deer in the headlights. I simply did not know what to say.

I can tell you my reason for waiting. I did not want to deal with it. I saw the annual review as a safe and formal opportunity to confront the employee. The other reason is, if you do not get on top of performance issues right away, they will only get worse. The final reason is the company will be negatively impacted. Every employee and what they are responsible for is important to the success of your company. Do not allow performance issues to persist.

I cannot stress this enough. Address performance issues as they emerge. Be consistent. Address them routinely. Address them in your weekly check-ins with your employees. Address them in the annual review. I also suggest doing a mid-year review for all of your employees. This is not only for the purpose of correcting performance issues, but making sure your employees are on track with meeting their goals. It is also an opportunity for you to find out what resources or help they may need to achieve their goals.

Coach Them Up or Coach Them Out

Every organization has A players, B players and C players. Your A players are your ideal employees. They are trusted, competent, loyal and hard workers. They not only perform well, but they fit your company's values and they contribute to a positive workplace culture. These are the kinds of people you want to hire and retain.

Your B players are good employees, but they are the diamonds in the rough. They have great character, work hard, but they have some growing to do. The good news is that B players can become A players, but not if left to themselves. You have to invest in them and develop them.

How do you develop B players? This should apply to all of your employees, but what I am going to recommend is especially true for your B players. You develop them by investing in them and enriching them.

Professional development is the way to invest in your employees. They will feel valued, plus you are building their skills which will ultimately enhance the culture and operations of your company. One way to do this is to hire a professional coach to work with them on building their skills. They will have the opportunity to meet regularly with a coach to discuss their growth areas and the coach will bring resources to the coaching partnership to develop them. Coaching is powerful because the employee gets to do some evaluation of where they are, grow in self-awareness and set professional goals. Professional coaches also hold them accountable for meeting and even exceeding their goals.

Another way is to invest money for them to attend workshops and seminars. Giving your employees time off to participate in these learning opportunities will go a long way in strengthening your company. It is also important to bring in training facilitators to do workshops and seminars onsite for your teams.

There is a cost for doing these professional development activities. It will cost you money, so make sure this is a priority in your budget. It will cost time because it will require them being away from their responsibilities to engage in them. Trust me, the benefits outweigh the time away.

Personal growth is the top driver of developing work-related skills. Workers, in general, want to develop their work-related skills. Many employees have to take their learning and development into their own hands. This may work for your high initiative employees. Many of your employees will not do this, so you, as the leader of your organization, have to provide the structure and opportunities for their learning and growth.

Be sure you work with your direct reports on setting up a wellness plan. Emphasize self-care and life balance. Not only should you emphasize and encourage it, be intentional about helping them establish a plan. Make sure you check in with them to see how they are doing. They will need accountability, especially your A players as they can be workaholics and neglect self-care. You have to make sure they are taking care of themselves.

For every annual performance evaluation, I have employees write specific and measurable goals for their professional development and well being. I suggest some things and I ask them what they need to do to grow and exercise self-care. After we agree on the goals, these goals actually go into their review document and I check up on them quarterly. Often, I check up on them in my weekly check-ins.

Did you know that 76% of workers experienced at least one mental health symptom in the past year? And 70% of those in top management are seriously quitting for a job that better supports their well being. Now, 81% of employees are saying that improving their well being is more important than advancing their work. The sad point is the research shows that employees are not receiving this kind of support. In fact, 70% feel that their employers are not doing enough to prevent or alleviate burnout within their organizations.

In regards to your A and B players, if you prioritize professional development and well being, you will greatly enhance their job performance. There is also the long-term benefit of retaining them. They will want to stay with your company. Continue to coach your A and B players up so they will remain in a growing and learning mode.

Now, what about your C players? The bottom line is you have to coach them *out*. They are not the right fit for your organization. They are the wrong individuals on the bus. Obviously, as you navigate this, you have to follow best practices and legal procedures.

Best practices include communicating and reinforcing the expectations and desired outcomes, documenting their performance behaviors and providing opportunities for them to improve. This involves performance improvement plans, coaching them up and investing in their professional development to grow. You need to demonstrate that you have made every effort to help them succeed.

Sometimes, it comes down to termination if they do not improve or demonstrate the willingness to improve. Every company needs a good HR person and an employment attorney. If you have to terminate an employee, make sure that you seek the counsel and advice of an employment attorney. This type of legal counsel will protect your organization from legal exposure and liability, which can cost the company a lot of money.

Do not tolerate performance issues that will have a negative impact on your company. Many leaders either ignore them or do not handle them properly. Be sure you address them but do so in the right way.

CHAPTER 6

COMMUNICATION PROBLEMS

Let me tell you about a mistake I made a few years ago. Not only was it a mistake, but it was one of my most embarrassing moments as a leader. My administrative team and I decided we needed to change our CRM. I researched different systems and platforms; I really did my homework. I spoke with representatives on the phone, tested their platforms and researched the reviews. I narrowed it down to three CRMs that might be a good fit for our operations.

I met with two individuals from the administrative team and shared my findings and recommendations. I asked them to run with it. My first mistake was not asking them to keep me in the loop. These individuals were two of my most competent direct reports. I trusted them. One of my weaknesses as a leader is I have always implicitly trusted competent employees. I knew that these two individuals would get the job done.

The first thing I asked them to do was to take my three recommendations and come back to me with their final choice, and then we would sign the deal with the company, execute the training and do the migration of information. Weeks went by and I did not hear from them. They were quietly working together behind the scenes. Finally, they came back to me with their final decision and I approved. My second mistake was that I never checked back in and they never checked back with me.

I had a very busy executive position with multiple responsibilities, so I was focused on other duties. They also knew I trusted them so they did not feel the need to check-in with me about any updates or where we were in the process.

One afternoon, sitting in my office, one of the ladies called me indicated that we were at the deadline. In order to begin the deal with the company we had selected, the contract had to be signed; otherwise, it would be nullified. Keep in mind, I had taken my hands off the project and there was very little communication between me and my direct reports.

The company faxed the contract over to me and, without even reading the contract, I signed, dated and sent it back to the company. I thought everything was fine. We later learned that the contract was not in our favor. It was a long-term contract and there were fees that I, at least, was not aware of. I signed it without even reading it because I trusted that my direct reports had asked all the right questions and received the information we needed. There had not been any communication about the specifics of the contract with my direct reports. We were stuck with a bad contract.

The embarrassing part was later in the month, when I met with our Finance Committee members, everyone gave me a very hard time. No, they didn't reprimand or criticize me. They made jokes about me signing a bad deal. One of the members of the committee laughed and said, "The next time we have to do a contract, let's make sure we read it and let's make sure that Reggie doesn't sign it." They all chuckled, myself included. Even though it was a joking moment, I was embarrassed. I was embarrassed because I prided myself on being a good manager and administrator.

A better decision would have been made if there had been better communication. Communication is the strength of an organization and communication can be the weakness of an organization. Relationships are about good communication. That is not just true in our personal lives, but our professional lives as well. If you want your company to run smoothly, you have to have a good communication system.

Communication breakdowns can be disastrous. These breakdowns can create an unhealthy culture, erode relationships and have a negative impact on your operational systems.

Communication Barriers

Even though communication is one of your most important resources, it is not easy to attain. It is based on relationships and is fostered through time, effort and transparency. Open and transparent communication helps employees feel more satisfied in their work and will help achieve the goals of your company through collaboration.

If you are going to run an effective business, you have to be proactive, diligent and intentional about removing the communication barriers. Communication involves encoding and decoding. There is always a sender and receiver. We have to be aware of how information is filtered and any potential barriers.

First, there is the busyness barrier. Every company I have consulted with runs in the fast lane. Everyone has demands, deadlines and sometimes more work than they have time. In those cases, we have a tendency to rush through our work. One of the things we ignore is the value of good communication. It takes time out of our day when we have to pause and provide and receive information that is going to help us do our work. But you must understand that it is not time wasted. It is valuable. Even though it takes time, it is important to invest in communicating and collaborating with your colleagues. Start to view communication as a part of your work

Second, there is the barrier of how we communicate. The Covid-19 pandemic has changed the landscape of how we do business. During the shut down, we began communicating solely through video and messaging platforms. We lost that personal touch. Even though we have opened up our world again, we now have a hybrid approach. You have members of your team who now work in-person and some who work remotely. You may even have a rotational system that allows everyone to have a few days in person and a few days remote. This has changed our interaction. I facilitated a number of meetings online during the pandemic. I am an observer of people and their behaviors, and I noticed that some people just weren't as engaged.

Third, there is the barrier of impersonal communication. I love technology. It is designed to help us work faster and more efficiently. Besides the loss of personal interaction, there is the issue of not knowing how to use the technology. Many companies have implemented many platforms for providing and receiving important information. What I am talking about are platforms and drives that maintain information. Often, employees are forced to go to those platforms to get information. My word of advice to you is make sure that you train your people on how to use these tools and platforms. If they do not have the knowledge or are unfamiliar with them, they simply will not use them.

There are also people barriers. Every organization has information hoarders. They like to keep information to themselves. They consider themselves the "gatekeepers." They see information as power. The problem is this keeps everyone else in the dark about direction, decisions, policies, practices and procedures. This is what I call a communication block. Information stops at one person, which affects achieving the mission of the organization.

Another people barrier that we all sometime struggle with is active listening. Experts in the field of communication talk about physical noise and psychological noise. The noises around us and within us keep us from properly listening. Physical noise includes external distractions. Someone is talking with you and you are distracted by someone in the next cubicle or the conversation they are having on the phone seems more interesting than the person talking to you.

Psychological noise is internal. It is your filter. You become distracted by emotional factors. Maybe you have a personal issue going on and that affects your filter. Maybe you don't like the person you're talking to, so you selectively listen or you rush the communication. If this is a regular practice for you, then you are missing essential information for your work and the success of the company.

I want to spend some time talking about active listening. Communication is a two-way street. It involves talking and listening. My wife is a big fan of the Judge Judy show and sometimes I'll watch with her. Judge Judy has been known for saying, "You have one mouth and two ears." The idea is we should *listen* more than we talk.

Active listening involves being attentive. It is listening to understand. We often listen to respond and we miss what the other person is saying. I have known people to listen for points that they can challenge or respond back on. They find one statement that they hold on to and they do not hear the entire message that the speaker is communicating. Listen carefully when your colleagues are speaking with you and listen to understand what they are saying.

Ask questions for clarification. Again, some people ask questions to challenge other people. In the work environment, it is about making sure that you understand them. You not only want to listen to what they are saying, but what they are not saying.

This is emotional listening. After the other person communicates their message, if something is not clear to you, ask questions that will allow them to clarify.

One of my practices is to paraphrase what the other person has said. That has been interesting. Sometimes, I am spot on. However, there have been times when the other person has said to me, "no, that is not what I am saying at all." I will then ask them for further clarification until I get it right. Paraphrasing to the other person lets them know you were truly listening whether you got it right or not. Sometimes we don't get it because of the person's communication style. It's not that they are poor communicators. It's more that their style is different than yours. Sometimes it is your filter that creates a lack of understanding.

Psychological Safety

As the leader of your organization, team or work group, this is where you can demonstrate leadership. One of the things that great leaders do is they model the behavior they want from their employees. Leaders set culture in the organization. A huge part of culture is how your employees relate to each other.

Psychological safety is an essential component for high team performance. It creates an environment of authenticity and transparency. People will feel comfortable sharing their ideas and perspectives. The more input you can receive from your employees, the better your company will be. Unfortunately, there are so many smart people in the workplace who shut down and remain quiet in meetings because they do not believe they will be heard. Often, they feel they will be criticized for their thoughts, so they stay in their safe place and remain quiet.

Psychological safety in the workplace is the value that all employees can speak up and share opinions without experiencing repercussions. This starts with the leader. When an employee comes to you with an idea, be sure to listen to them, thank them for their ideas and evaluate if it is something that will enhance the company.

I once worked for a senior leader who always responded with the negative. He would shoot holes in everyone's ideas. Naturally, the team stopped bringing ideas to him. I was the number two guy in the organization in charge of operations, managing the staff and overseeing the programs. And even I shut down. I eventually got to the point where I simply would say to him, "You make the decision, tell me what you want and I will execute." My role shifted from being a fellow decision maker to an executor because I got tired of always having solutions and ideas shot down. The entire team felt the same because we had a leader who did not truly listen and model a safe and open environment for people to communicate. I have to say, the organization was less than what it could have been because of his micromanaging leadership style.

Effective Communication Systems

We have discussed creating a culture or environment for healthy communication, which involves breaking down barriers. Now, I want to get very practical and share some steps. These steps revolve around meetings.

Meetings! Meetings! Meetings! I am sure you get tired of going to so many meetings. I do believe that some companies have way too many meetings. What is worse is so many meetings are run poorly. They do not have an objective. In my past roles, I have often felt we were meeting just for the sake of meeting.

Meetings do have a purpose. For one, meetings can be instrumental in team building. They are also designed for evaluation of the work, planning the work and creating goals for achieving the mission and vision of the organization. They are extremely important... but they have to be managed *effectively*.

I have always managed meetings by having an intentional structure to foster communication. Weekly meetings generally included one-on-ones with my direct reports. These meetings fostered healthy relationships between me and the team members, giving us the opportunity to communicate important things about their specific part in achieving the work of the organization.

I also had monthly meetings. These were meetings with the entire staff to pass on important information. I also had monthly meetings with the board and the finance teams. These meetings were critical to the running of the organizations where I served as a senior leader and provided opportunities to keep everyone informed so good decisions could be made.

I also suggest having informal meetings. I always loved what I called standup meetings. I would gather the people who needed to be involved in collaboration and decision making. We would not sit down in my office, a boardroom or conference room. Sometimes we would meet in my office, a hallway or the middle of the administrative suite. We would not sit. We would all stand and chat over important matters.

These meetings were no longer than 20 minutes. We'd check up on each other regarding projects and schedules for the week. I would also ask them what they needed from me in terms of support and resources. After the brief check in, we would go back to our offices to resume our work. I encourage you as a leader to check in with your employees often. This is not to breathe down their necks as a micromanager, but to demonstrate that you care about them and their work; find out how you can support them. It is also a chance for you to receive valuable feedback and information from them.

The biggest problem in most organizations is that we operate on assumptions. We assume that everyone has all the information. We assume that others know what we know. Often, they do not. Be intentional about creating a safe environment in your organization that will allow the natural and powerful flow of information. Communicate with your employees and team members often. Don't be afraid to over communicate. Don't ever assume that people are getting the information the first time or even a few times. Be consistent in your communication system.

CHAPTER 7

LEADING PEOPLE WHO DON'T WANT TO BE LED

I once had a very competent employee who loved the organization, was great at her specific job and was extremely responsible and reliable. But there was a problem that created frustration for me. She wasn't open to the ideas of others, even mine. What was really frustrating was I would give her specific instructions about what I wanted, but she would often do it her way.

She also got involved in things that were outside of her job description. I would often tell her to stay in her lane. She was argumentative and could be very difficult to work with. Sometimes, her work was neglected because she was so busy getting into everyone else's business in the office. She felt she needed to have input in work that was not related to her job description.

Needless to say, she was difficult to lead. Other staff members found her difficult to work with. Maybe you are struggling with people like that in your organization. You are wondering what to do with these individuals. You're asking how to manage them. If so, this chapter is just for you.

Characteristics of People Difficult To Lead

They think they are the smartest person in the room. They have an attitude of superiority. They have the *best* ideas. It is their way or the highway. They challenge other team members in meetings constantly. They even refuse to take instructions from you, the leader.

Now, don't get me wrong. As the leader, you need to be willing to listen to all of your employees, even your most difficult ones. Hear them out, ask questions and share what you want and need. Collaborate with them. Obviously, if their way seems the best direction to go in, then affirm it, embrace it and implement it.

I have made mistakes with employees like this, even the one I mentioned in my story. Looking in the rearview mirror, I look back with regrets. Sometimes I found myself giving in to them because they exhausted me. I just wanted to be done with the discussion and move on. What I found was that giving in to them did not always produce the best results. In fact, there were times when caving in led to major mistakes. Sometimes, it is necessary to go with your head and your gut. In the past, with some of my direct reports, I have gone against my better judgment because they were so pushy. Again, if their ideas are better than yours, then go with it. But if you know if it is *not* best then, as the leader, make the decision that needs to be made.

Leadership can be hard at times. *What do leaders do?* They make the hard decisions. Sometimes, you have to make decisions that are not popular. You have to be OK with that. At the end of the day, you are the one responsible for decisions and the outcomes. Don't allow your employees to bully you because they have a sense of superior knowledge.

As a leader, you have a big picture view. Most of the time, your employees do not see the full picture. They not only see it from their perspective, but they see it from their *position*. They are not involved in every department or aspect of your company. You know things that they don't– things that are important to making the *right* decisions.

Another characteristic of this kind of employee is they want to be in charge. They have control issues. They are "self-appointed" leaders. As a consultant, I have had the opportunity to watch this in action. In meetings, weaker leaders will defer to these employees. I have watched this time and time again. What I have noticed is the person being deferred to is usually the loudest and most opinionated person in the room. Even though the positional leader is in charge on paper, sometimes there is an unofficial leader.

Unofficial leaders emerge because they have been allowed to take control. They have had their way over and over because the leader became exhausted. The problem with this is your team will begin to look to this person, diminishing your role as the leader.

They also have a way of monopolizing meetings. I teach seminars on meeting management and I talk about the different types of people who interact together on a team. There is always the "talkative one." This person never shuts up. They dominate the conversation. On every agenda item, they have something to say. If this is not managed, you will not hear from other members of the team. Because they can be opinionated, it will shut down others in the room and you will not get the collaboration and input necessary to move forward.

The characteristic that can be most frustrating is they will make decisions on their own. They do this without running their thoughts by anyone, including you. You then are caught by surprise when you hear of it and the results of their decision. They have a disrespect of leadership because they really want to be the one in charge.

Beware of Coalitions

People who are difficult to lead can create coalitions. They will sometimes use tactics of manipulation. They do this to obtain a following which can undermine your leadership. They build alliances to get support for what they want to do by going behind your back.

The way I have seen this played out is they will move around the office and talk to others about their ideas and opinions, in an effort to secure support. Sometimes you might see three or four people in an office behind closed doors and this person is right in the middle of it. This often happens before meetings, after the agenda has been mailed out in preparation for the meeting. This is to develop a strategy for getting support for the decision that they want to see made.

Sometimes, this person will get a group of people together after a meeting if the results of the meeting do not go in their favor. I didn't fall off the turnip truck this morning. I can tell you exactly what is going on in this unofficial meeting. Two things are happening. They are criticizing the leader and the outcomes of the meeting. Some of your employees will actually support this person, which will undermine your influence as a leader. If another employee is not aware of what the person is doing, it could make you appear inadequate as a leader.

They are not only criticizing the leadership, but they are trying to get support for sabotaging what was decided in the meeting. I have mentioned the importance of a healthy culture in organizations. This can create dysfunction in your teams and entire organization, so you have to address it.

Confronting People Who Are Difficult To Lead

Unfortunately, as leaders, we sometimes move into management roles and we have a team made up of people we did not choose. Sometimes, there are some you would not have chosen to be a part of your team. Many times, you will inherit people who are difficult to lead.

Leaders approach me about this problem often. The first thing I tell them is to listen and look for the hidden emotional need. These kinds of employees are lacking something or looking for something. I am not a psychologist or therapist, so I won't go into a psychological analysis of how they are wired. I will say, however, there is an emotional need that is unmet that has absolutely nothing to do with you.

You need to understand that there is something that is driving their behavior and actions.

It is important that you take the high road when you confront them. This means treating them with respect and remaining calm. Whatever you do, do not react. Speak directly, but kindly. If you don't, they will use your reaction against you. If they have formed alliances, be assured that they will report that to their supporters. You will look bad as a leader, which will diminish your leadership influence with other employees. Avoid getting defensive and displaying anger. Stay professional in your conversations with them.

Conversations with this type of employee can be emotionally charged. Keep your emotions down. Learn ways to stand up to them with confidence and resist the urge to attack back. This will help you navigate emotionally charged situations and conversations.

Have these conversations privately. *What if they disrespectfully challenge you in a meeting?* First, address it. Your team will be watching how you handle it. You need to show strength and courage so that you do not lose leadership credibility. You also need to be calm and in control so that your team members do not lose respect for you.

The next thing you need to do is stay focused on the issue; not on the person attacking you. At that moment, they are challenging you about a proposal or a decision. Be rational, logical and answer their concerns with solid rationales. If they take the low road and go personal, you take the high road by keeping the focus on the issue. Address the issue. Don't attack the person. If you have solid reasons for your decisions and well-thought-out rationales for your proposals, drive those points home.

Your Management Style Is Important

Everyone has a default management style. That is the style that we are most comfortable with, fits our personality and is the one we use in supervising people. Your management style is the way you manage individuals, groups, projects and meetings. Your style also demonstrates how you organize work, make decisions and use your authority.

There are many styles of leadership and management. Even though you have your own unique style, it is important to know when to use other styles. Your style should be customized to fit the people, groups or situations you are dealing with at the moment.

For the purposes of the topic of this chapter, I want to mention two of those styles. There is the *collaborative* style and the *authoritative* style. As a good leader, the collaborative style is the one we should try to use most of the time. With this style, a manager's decision-making process is influenced by their employees. Managers work closely with their team members in making decisions. This builds trust with your employees and provides you with the best feedback for making good decisions. The use of this style will often result in you making the final decision, but it is done so in consultation with other team members.

The authoritative style generally is not a good style to default to all the time. It does not foster a healthy culture. It is one that micromanages people and the leader makes decisions all alone. If this is your default style, you will not build cohesive and healthy teams. It is the autocratic style and employees find it oppressive.

There are times when the authoritative style is effective. It is effective when dealing with people who are difficult to lead. Keep your attitude in a good place. It is not so much that you are saying, "It is my way or the highway." In the case of working with this kind of employee, it is simply communicating that this is the decision you are making and sharing the reason for it. After a while, that employee will slowly discover that you are no pushover and you will not be bullied. It also instills confidence in your other employees because they will know clearly who the leader is. It will enhance the trust and credibility of your leadership with others in the organization. They will know that the authoritative style is not your normal way of supervising, but they will have the confidence to know that you will use it when you have to.

Let me close this chapter with a conversation I had with my wife before writing it. I was sharing with my wife, Jeannine, about what I was going to be writing and asked for her input. I did so because she and I represent two different sides of leadership.

I have always been a senior leader and have had to manage people who are difficult to lead. She has been in the workforce for as long as I have. The only difference is she has never been a senior leader. She has worked for a number of senior leaders and she has watched some of them not navigate these kinds of employees well. She has watched bosses be manipulated, controlled and bullied. She has watched fellow colleagues take over because some of her bosses did not have the strength and courage to manage and confront people who are difficult to lead.

I asked her how it made her feel. Her answer was insightful. She said she has lost respect for some of her previous bosses. She also said that it lowered her morale and she has watched the culture of some of her teams erode because of the way those people were managed. My word of advice and caution to you as a leader? You cannot afford to lose leadership credibility as you'll risk stifling overall employee morale which will negatively impact the culture of your organization.

CHAPTER 8

GETTING DIVERSITY AND INCLUSION RIGHT

I had an insightful learning experience with a company recently struggling with issues of race, equity, inclusion and diversity. There were different ethnic groups within the organization. Because of the representation, there was obviously diversity, but some of the groups did not feel valued and included. I decided to conduct listening sessions intended to create a safe and courageous space for everyone to share their experiences and perspectives.

I felt this would be a great first step and opportunity because it created an environment of better understanding for each other. My learning was when people are given a structure to open up and they feel comfortable and safe, they will communicate in a healthy manner. It also allowed the different groups to have a mutual appreciation and respect for each other. You probably have already guessed what's coming next. This greatly enhanced the culture of the organization and the way the employees worked together.

I am a black man who grew up in a small rural town in west Tennessee. I grew up in the 60s and 70s and experienced racial insensitivity and and discrimination. The town that I grew up in did not have a lot of diversity. It was primarily white and black people, with the black population being the minority.

My goal was to integrate. I had white friends, played sports and participated in school activities. Often, I was the only or among a few blacks involved in social and athletic activities. I even was a statistic at times by being the first black to ever do certain things. Even though I got involved, I did not always feel included and accepted.

My professional career has not been any different. I have worked for a number of organizations where I was one of few minorities or people of color. I experienced implicit bias and microaggressions. I will explain those terms later in this chapter. I had to take the initiative to be included. Often, the organization did not make the effort to make me feel like I belonged. I had to do it on my own and I worked hard to integrate into the culture of those organizations.

I also discovered that some of those organizations did things to make the minority groups feel included, but those efforts were done uninformed. These organizations ended up doing the wrong things and even saying the wrong things. The intentions, I believe, were noble. The approaches were done without the proper education and information.

If you are in the business world, you have probably noticed that organizations today are addressing race, justice, diversity and equity. This emphasis has been elevated due to some of the unrest we have seen over the past few years. The events that highlighted issues were the 2020 shootings of Tanisha Anderson, Rayshard Brooks, Michael Brown, Breonna Taylor, George Floyd and others.

These recent events have shown that race is a topic that has been long overdue. I have to be honest with you - this topic is a difficult one because it is highly sensitive and emotional. Everyone has a different perspective and life experience. It is important to note that the unrest around race has prompted many organizations in the United States to evaluate their systems. Unfortunately, business leaders do not know where to begin in making sure that their organizations get issues of diversity and inclusion right.

Organizations are in the process of launching initiatives to address these issues. In fact, many companies have created a new department or division called the "Office of Diversity and Equity." They have hired officers to lead these departments. Some companies have even made this position a part of their C-suite. The purpose of these offices is to address institutional policies and practices that do not foster equity, justice and inclusion.

Let's Look at Some Terms

One of the things organizations need to do is evaluate where they are and how they are doing in this area. That can be an internal process, but a number of organizations are hiring consultants to come in and conduct an organizational audit to discover biases. There are two types of biases.

The first type is "explicit" bias. This is based on assumptions and judgments influenced by stereotypes, prejudice and personal experiences. Expressions of this type of bias are intentional and overt. These have been minimized in organizations due to laws and legal orders. Organizations cannot get away with overt biases today because of legal consequences.

The second type is "implicit" bias. This is based on automatic assumptions and quick judgments without awareness and intention. These are covert and hidden. An organization can have unfair policies and practices without even being aware of them.

This is why an organizational audit conducted by a professional experienced consultant could help your organization. As a leader, you are in your organization and it is easy to view it through a narrow lens. Consultants, on the other hand, come in with an outside view, providing objectivity. They will see things that you, as the leader, may not see.

Another term you need to consider is "microaggressions." This term was coined by Harvard University psychiatrist, Chester M. Pierce, in 1970 to describe insults and dismissals. Microaggressions are verbal or behavioral slights. Sometimes they are intentional and sometimes they are not. Either way, they communicate hostile, derogatory or negative attitudes toward culturally marginalized groups of people.

There are behavioral microaggressions. These are literal acts of racism against a particular group. An example of this kind of microaggression would be individuals spreading misinformation about COVID-19 by placing the blame on Asia. This misinformation created hate against Asian Americans.

There are verbal microaggressions. It can be a phrase or statement, intentional or unintentional that are negative prejudicial slights or insults. Sometimes they take the form of what I call a backhanded compliment. My wife and I both have experienced this in our careers. Years ago, one of my wife's colleagues told her that she is pretty "for a black woman." I am a public communicator. I had a man once tell me that I speak well "for a black man."

Do you see the verbal microaggressions in both examples? They were both backhanded compliments. Both individuals compliment my wife and me, but it was based on the faulty assumption that black women are not pretty and black people cannot speak well. I am sad to report that this does go on in the workplace. I consult with many companies and I have heard a number of people of color share experiences like this.

Diversity Is More Than Representation

I live and work in Southern California where there are many ethnic and cultural groups. When you walk into most companies, you will see a representation of many of these groups. By way of definition, diversity is a mix or a specific collection of people. It is about variety; not about quotas, statistics and numbers.

True diversity celebrates the mix of people in your organization. It is respecting the various groups in the organization. The differences of the various collections of groups must be accepted, embraced and respected. *Why is this important?* Diversity provides the benefit of having a broader range of perspectives, experiences and opinions. Your company will be much more effective if you tap into what each group brings in terms of knowledge, skills and experience.

Diversity will improve the reputation of your company. Companies that value and prioritize diversity make all of their employees feel welcomed, which makes the company more efficient and effective. Happy employees are more likely to be loyal and committed to the company and their respective roles. It will also enhance your company's reputation with customers, investors and stakeholders. You will widen your recruitment opportunities and improve performance from your employees. A 2018 Randstad Study found that 78% of employees valued workplace equity and diversity. Millennials value this more than the generations before them. This means that the future success of your company depends on getting this right. Many prospective employees do their research to see how companies manage diversity and equity. If you are doing a good job of this, you will recruit good employees and retain them. This is all a part of having a healthy workplace culture.

Don't Miss the Importance of Inclusion

It is not enough to just "be diverse." I have heard executives brag about their statistics and the mix of groups within their organizations. When you take a deeper dive, you might find that inclusion is missing.

Inclusion is the secret sauce. This is the extent to which diverse groups are able to fully participate and contribute. This means giving a seat at the table for everyone.

As a consultant, I have found that many organizations have the numbers and the representation, but inclusion is missing in layers of the organization. Many of my organizational audits have found that there is no diversity in the senior leadership team, the C-suite and on the board. There needs to be shared power in the organization. You not only need representation in the people who make the sausage for your company; you also need representation from all groups in the decision-making structure. This is true inclusion. Everyone feels welcome and everyone has the opportunity to shape the organization in a significant way.

When I submit consultant reports and highlight this problem for leadership teams, the leaders will present a problem to me. Since I am a black consultant, they will often tell me that we want more black employees, more black senior leaders and more blacks in our C-suite. Then, they will share with me their recruiting practices, often saying they have made every effort to recruit qualified black employees and leaders. My answer often surprises them. I will tell them that they do not have a recruitment problem. Instead, they have a networking problem.

I advise them to network with black colleges, graduate schools, Black Chamber of Commerces and other places where they can find qualified people. What they do not understand is that they have to build relationships with entities that train and work with black professionals. This strategy will work for all ethnic and cultural groups. You don't recruit the employees you need to build a diverse organization by posting job openings. You have to be intentional about networking with different organizations where you can find qualified and diverse individuals.

Company Values That Promote Diversity and Inclusion

Values are the deep-seated beliefs and behaviors of an organization. They drive the organization. If you are going to have a healthy organization, you need to set values that promote diversity and inclusion.

Awareness is an important value. It is important to be aware of your own personal biases. We all have them. Self-aware people acknowledge their issues, including their inappropriate expressions toward other groups of people.

It is also important to be aware of your organization's issues. This could be the personal biases that some of your employees have. These need to be addressed. More than likely, your company may have systems, policies and practices that do not foster healthy relations between the various groups in your organization.

Listening is a value that needs to be embraced. I have been hired by organizations to facilitate listening sessions around race, diversity, equity and inclusion. Recently, I worked with an organization where I worked with another consultant who was white. The synergy between us was amazing. It also created a positive dynamic that led to some good discussions. We did a series of three sessions and we experienced various cultural groups discussing with respect their views on these issues. This resulted in a better workplace environment.

I worked with another company alongside the same consultant as a partner. We met our match. The tension and emotions were high. The different racial and ethnic groups did not mix very well. The group of people didn't listen to each other. They were argumentative. They did not validate each other's life and work experiences. It was a nightmare leading that group. Unfortunately, after we finished consulting with the company, the company's culture continued to erode, there were resignations and terminations and the company got completely sidetracked in achieving its mission and vision.

What was the difference? The absence of listening for understanding is the simple answer. Two other necessary values are learning and empathy. You have to come into these conversations with a desire to learn as much as possible about the norms and culture of other groups. It is important to ask insightful questions so that you have a better understanding of how they think and view the world. This is very important in the workplace. A person's worldview determines how a person works, so it is beneficial to have that kind of knowledge. Sometimes, you have to listen and ask questions to get that information.

Empathy is essential. As you listen to the stories and life experiences of others, you will find pain. You need to express empathy. After the murder of George Floyd, I engaged in many race conversations with my white friends. I shared my experiences with personal and systemic racism. I always appreciated my friends when they expressed understanding and compassion for what I have gone through. I had others that downplayed or tried to convince me that what I experienced was not real. I have to admit that hearing those kinds of comments was hurtful. You lead people with different life experiences. Listen to them and learn from them. Share your experiences and perspectives and encourage them to try to understand your perspective.

Some Practical Takeaways

I would encourage you to begin with a Diversity & Inclusion Organizational Assessment. You may not be comfortable with the findings, but I assure you that you cannot change your organization unless you get this important analysis. You don't know what you don't know until you *do know*.

Set up listening sessions to hear from your employees. Biases are not only personal and interpersonal; they are also institutional and structural. Institutional biases are discriminatory treatment, unfair practices and inequitable opportunities that impact the organization. Your Policies & Procedural Manual may be well written, but your policies may be negatively impacting the dynamics of diversity and inclusion. Your employees will tell you if they think something is not in their favor or best interest. It will be to your advantage to listen, learn and change the things that are keeping your company from a healthy inclusive workplace culture.

Develop a "Diversity, Equity & Inclusion" statement that defines your beliefs and practices around these issues. These statements begin with an acknowledgment of issues that are not fair. They include what you believe how things should be. They conclude with actions that you are going to take. I had the opportunity to review many statements of organizations after the murder of George Floyd. Some of them were empty because they were fluff. They did not include a call to action. These statements should address your internal policy and public policy.

Keep in mind that not only is your employment team diverse, but our society at large as well. Your customers are a part of the larger community. As you understand your team, you will also understand your customers. Your customers will have a deeper appreciation for the work that you are attempting to do in the diversity and inclusion area. Studies have shown that companies with above average diversity and inclusion focus have higher revenue.

Make changes in the policies and practices that are not fostering positivity in diversity and inclusion. Most companies undergo extensive strategic planning processes. I suggest making diversity and equity a priority in your strategic focus. Set goals and action plans in this area.

Finally, set up professional training for diversity and inclusion. Diversity training in the past has not been effective. The reason for that is it only addresses it from a legal perspective and it was all about compliance. Companies take their employees through this to minimize legal exposure. They want their employees to know what creates legal liability for the company. This is important. I am not underestimating the value of this, but take your training further by bringing in the human and relational aspect of diversity and inclusion.

I encourage you to take your company on this exciting journey. You will not always get it right. You are going to make mistakes. Many companies do nothing because they do not know what to do or they fear they might do the wrong thing. Your employees will appreciate the fact that you are a champion of diversity and inclusion. If you listen to their feedback and hire a professional consultant, you will achieve the goals you need to reach. Keep in mind that it is a journey, not a destination. Keep learning, growing and changing.

CONCLUSION

I was in my mid-twenties and it was early in my professional career. At the time, I was not in a senior leadership position. I was a staff member; the youngest on the team. In our weekly staff meetings, our custom was to go around the table and report to the others details of the previous week's accomplishments and goals. One of my colleagues, in his report, brought up something that hit a nerve with our senior leader. When he did, the rest of us knew that this was the wrong topic to bring up and it was certainly not the right time.

I had much respect for our senior leader. After my colleague finished with his report, our senior leader hit the roof. He was extremely angry at my colleague. He was yelling, banging on the table and used some shocking language. I was surprised at the entire scene– surprised my colleague was foolish enough to bring up the particular issue and also by the response of our senior leader.

At the time, I did not take a leadership lesson away from that experience. In fact, I have, at times, blown up with colleagues and direct reports the same way as this senior leader did. Years later, as I reflected on that experience, I came to realize that leaders must control their emotions. Boy, I wish I had learned that earlier in my career.

I believe that emotional intelligence is one of the most important characteristics in leading businesses and organizations. As you deal with people issues and problems in your organization, your response to them is important. You cannot control how people behave, but you do have control over your emotional responses.

Self-Awareness

As a young leader, I was not self-aware. Self-awareness is a key ingredient in leading with emotional intelligence. It is certainly a key ingredient for dealing with difficult people in your organization. Self-awareness means having a good understanding of your emotions. That sounds easy, but that statement is empty without some practical applications. So, what exactly does it mean to be self-aware as a leader? Ask yourself three questions.

The first question is, *what emotion gives me the most problems in my business relationships?* For years, mine was anger. I could easily blow my top if employees did not do their jobs, showed up late for work or did not complete projects on time. I was unaware that I struggled with anger. Be honest with yourself and identify the specific emotion that negatively affects your influence as a leader.

The next two questions have to do with triggers. *What kinds of situations create these feelings in me?* As a leader, you deal with multiple situations, and there are specific situations that draw out inappropriate emotional responses for you. You need to identify those triggers so you can prepare for them.

The final question is also a trigger question *What types of people or personalities trigger this emotion in me?* Over the years, I have learned the types of people who bring out anger in me. I have come to realize that, in the workplace, you cannot avoid or ignore them. You still have to work with them. One of my strategies is to anticipate what they might say in meetings or how they may respond to a conversation with me. I do this so that I am not caught off guard. I have to confess that I am not the best version of myself when my trigger personalities do what they do best irritate and agitate. To this day, I still do not do well with them.

I have grown in my emotional intelligence skills. Another strategy is to rehearse how I am going to respond. When I go into meetings with my trigger personalities, I just expect them to be themselves. I create a mental scenario of what they might do or say, and then I decide how I am going to respond. This puts me in a position of *responding* to them rather than *reacting* to them.

Managing Your Emotions

Emotional intelligence does not come from suppressing your emotions. It is acknowledging what you are feeling and then channeling your feelings in a positive and constructive direction. It is important to understand the nature of emotions. We are creatures of emotions. We have the capacity to really feel and express emotions.

The problem is how emotions are often channeled and directed. Some people suppress them, which is not healthy. Others feel the freedom to express them in unhealthy and unproductive ways. Emotional intelligence is understanding that you cannot act on impulse. You cannot react in the moment. That will destroy your leadership credibility. Leaders must control their emotions, not allow their emotions to control them and their behavior.

As a leader, you cannot demonstrate rage and anger when dealing with a difficult employee. Often leaders have to manage a crisis. You cannot respond with visible anxiety and panic. Leaders calm their teams and employees during times of crisis. They are looking to you for peace and stability. They will look to you for the assurance that everything is going to be OK. You never want your emotions to create panic in your employees. You may be shaken up inside, but you have to maintain your composure.

Managing Relationships

I think you will agree that relationships are complex in all areas of life. That is true in the business world. Managing relationships is a key competency in emotional intelligence. It is the most visible tool in leadership because it involves persuasion, conflict management skills, and collaboration. If you want to be successful in leading your company and managing relationships, you need to learn how to handle the emotions of others. Again, you cannot control another person's feelings or responses, but you can control the environment. In other words, as the leader, you cannot allow another employee to sabotage a meeting or other interactions in your company by their negative expressions of emotions.

Working with people can be tricky because people are often emotional, sensitive, and in some cases *difficult*. The leader must learn skills that will help them to navigate the complexities of relationships. Relating to your employees in an emotionally intelligent manner is not disingenuous or manipulative. Emotionally intelligent leaders lead out of authenticity and by acting from genuine feelings.

We have already mentioned the idea of "emotional hijacking" in a previous chapter. That is allowing your rational brain to be hijacked by your emotional brain. It is easy to allow this to happen when in a crisis situation, conflict, and emotionally charged conversation. As a leader, you cannot afford for this to happen.

Practical Tips

I have some good news for you. Your emotional intelligence skills can improve. I have coached a number of business leaders with low EQ skills who believed they could not change. Yes, you can change and improve our EQ skills.

A 1991 study published in *Science Magazine* changed what neurologists knew about the brain. For years, experts believed that the brain is frozen, unable to change. The findings of this new study included the fact that the brain is "plastic." The term used is "plasticity," meaning the brain is flexible. The good news from this study is that you and I can learn new skills. It just takes discipline and reinforcement.

The first tip I would offer to you as a business leader is to learn to practice what I teach in my workshops and seminars. It is what I call "the pause." Think before you respond. In emotionally-charged situations, you are naturally going to be emotional. In order to have a rational response, you need time to think about it.

The second tip is to know your triggers. Know the kinds of situations and people that can lead you to hijack your logical response and your leadership credibility. Anticipate what could possibly be presented to you throughout the day and create a mental plan of how you are going to respond.

Third, practice empathy, which is a high and crucial EQ skill. One of my practices is to let people vent, even if they are venting because they are upset with me. As you listen without defensiveness, you are de-escalating the situations and you are bringing down their emotions. This also gives you time to bring down your emotions and think about your response.

If you are in business at any level, you have people problems. I want you to be encouraged as you complete this book. People problems are not fixed; they can be solved.

Solve them quickly. Do not let them fester. Address people problems as they come up. If you let them continue, they will only get worse and become much more difficult to resolve. Solve them strategically. Be thoughtful about how you go about solving them.

Take time to think through how you will confront difficult people and emotionally charged situations. Solve them relationally.

Remember, you are dealing with people with whom you have a relationship with. Even the difficult people in your organization have feelings and needs. Be honest and direct with them. Confront their behavior but be kind and respectful.

AUTHOR

Dr. Reggie Thomas – Resides in Chino Hills, California. Reggie's greatest strength is relationships. Over the years he has cultivated and nurtured multiple relationships at various levels of his life – both personally and professionally. His passion is to help leaders develop healthy relationships in the workplace as well as help individuals enjoy fulfilling and enriching relationships. Reggie holds a doctorate degree in Organizational Leadership and his doctoral dissertation focused on the importance of emotional intelligence in leadership. He has used that research to help scores of leaders improve their leadership skills and improve culture and morale in the workplace.

Reggie is President of PeakePotential, Inc. which is a firm that focuses on executive coaching, leadership coaching, training and consulting. He brings a wealth of experience in providing resources in the area of emotional intelligence, diversity and equity, team building, leadership, conflict management and building a healthy organization culture. Reggie is passionate about investing and pouring into other leaders. He is a "leader of leaders", who wants to see leaders reach their leadership potential. Reggie also has a passion for investing in others personally to improve the quality of their lives. Reggie offers help and resources to leaders regarding life balance, self-care, healthy relationships, setting boundaries, discovery of life purpose, legacy building and other life issues.

He is a gifted speaker and has been a speaker on a national basis for 32 years. He is available for keynote speeches, presentations, conferences, workshops and seminars. In addition to running his own company, he is also active in the community and serves on several boards.

Reggie wants his life legacy to be about serving others to help make their lives better. Nothing brings him more joy than celebrating the progress and success of others. Reggie has been married to Jeannine for 34 years and they have two grown daughters, Amanda and Emilee. He loves his family and takes pride in being a husband and father. Reggie and Jeannine enjoy traveling and over the past few years have broadened that interest by doing international travel. His goal is to visit as many countries as possible. Reggie is an avid runner. He has run 41 marathons and 6 ultra-marathons. He has also run the prestigious Boston Marathon 12 times.

www.ingramcontent.com/pod-product-compliance
Lightning Source LLC
LaVergne TN
LVHW041340080426
835512LV00006B/548